W9-BKN-777

PRO WRESTLING LEGENDS

Steve Austin
The Story of the Wrestler They Call "Stone Cold"

Bill Goldberg

Bret Hart
The Story of the Wrestler They Call "The Hitman"

The Story of the Wrestler
They Call "Hollywood" Hulk Hogan

Randy Savage
The Story of the Wrestler They Call "Macho Man"

The Story of the Wrestler They Call "Sting"

The Story of the Wrestler They Call "The Undertaker"

Jesse Ventura
The Story of the Wrestler They Call "The Body"

CHELSEA HOUSE PUBLISHERS

Jesse Ventura
The Story of the Wrestler
They Call "The Body"

Matt Hunter

Chelsea House Publi███
Philadelphia

Produced by Choptank Syndicate, Inc.

Editor and Picture Researcher: Mary Hull
Design and Production: Lisa Hochstein

CHELSEA HOUSE PUBLISHERS

Editor in Chief: Stephen Reginald
Managing Editor: James D. Gallagher
Production Manager: Pamela Loos
Art Director: Sara Davis
Director of Photography: Judy L. Hasday
Senior Production Editor: LeeAnne Gelletly
Cover Illustrator: Keith Trego

Cover Photos: Associated Press / Wide World Photos

The Chelsea House World Wide Web site
address is http://www.chelseahouse.com

3 5 7 9 8 6 4 2

Library of Congress Cataloging-in-Publication Data

Hunter, Matt.
    Jesse Ventura : the story of the wrestler they call "The Body"/ Matt Hunter.
        p. cm.—(Pro wrestling legends)
    Includes bibliographical references (p.) and index.
    Summary: A biography of Jesse "The Body" Ventura, the professional wrestler,
turned Hollywood action hero, turned radio talk show host who recently became
Governor of Minnesota.
    ISBN 0-7910-5410-1 (hc.) — ISBN 0-7910-5556-6 (pbk.)
    1. Ventura, Jesse   Juvenile literature. 2. Wrestlers—United States—Biography—
Juvenile literature. 3. Governors—Minnesota—Biography—Juvenile literature.
[1. Ventura, Jesse 2. Wrestlers. 3. Governors.]
    I. Title. II. Series.
GV1196.V46H86 1999
977.6'053'092—dc21
    [B]   99-34307
                                                                         CIP

Contents

1   "THE BODY" POLITIC

For a world used to hearing exaggeration coming from the mouth of Jesse "The Body" Ventura for many years, the statement "We shocked the world!" delivered before a cheering throng on the evening of November 3, 1998, was anything but exaggeration.

People were entertained when Ventura—the former professional wrestler, Hollywood action hero, and bombastic radio talk show host—announced that he was running for the office of governor of Minnesota. There are two very serious candidates in the race, they thought, but that's all right. Ventura will become a fun diversion in yet another year of politics as usual.

They never imagined he would win. Ventura never imagined he wouldn't. Still, the odds were stacked high against him.

The expected winner in the race for the highest office in the state was Democratic candidate Hubert "Skip" Humphrey III, the attorney general of Minnesota, and the son of Hubert H. Humphrey Jr., longtime Minnesota senator and the 38th vice president of the United States (from 1965 to 1969, under President Lyndon B. Johnson). Skip Humphrey's candidacy was boosted by the fact that he helped guide Minnesota to a

In 1998 Jesse Ventura was elected governor of Minnesota in a victory so remarkable the Associated Press called it "one of the most stunning political upsets of all time."

$6.1 billion-dollar victory in a lawsuit against the tobacco industry.

The second major candidate was Republican Norm Coleman, the mayor of St. Paul, the state capital of Minnesota. A former Democrat, Coleman was very popular in the state and had learned the ins and outs of state politics as a student of Skip Humphrey himself.

Then there was Jesse.

Running as a candidate from the Reform Party, Ventura was no stranger to politics. In 1990, he was elected mayor of Brooklyn Park, the sixth-largest city in Minnesota. In winning that office, he defeated James Krautkremer, a man who had been mayor for 18 years. Ventura served a four-year term, during which the crime rate went down and taxes didn't go up.

But running for governor is far different than running for mayor. There are larger responsibilities, of course, but a campaign takes money. Big money. Humphrey and Coleman had millions to spend, and both were established figures on the Minnesota political landscape.

When Ventura asked billionaire Ross Perot, the Reform Party founder, for financial assistance for his campaign, Perot refused. As a result, Ventura had to run his campaign on a relatively modest budget of about $500,000. But if charisma and personality were cash, Ventura would be a billionaire many times over.

Ventura was quickly able to position himself outside the traditional political system, and this move made him very attractive to Minnesota voters. In speeches across the state, Ventura was poised and personable. He spoke in plain language and directed his comments to the voters, while the other two candidates spoke in political language and often directed their comments toward the newspapers or the evening news.

It didn't hurt Ventura's campaign either that a large part of his celebrated pro wrestling career had been spent in Minnesota.

If Ventura sounded different than the other candidates, that was just the beginning. He looked different, too—a lot different. Standing 6'4" and weighing 250 pounds, Ventura struck an imposing presence, made all the more interesting by his choice of clothing, which often included snakeskin boots and leather jackets.

Oh, yes: the bald head and outsider's demeanor made him stand out, too.

Ventura's choice of clothing and his direct speaking style got the people's attention, but it was what he was saying that kept their attention and made people take him seriously. A large part of his appeal was that he was an outsider battling the traditional political system (and there are plenty of people who like to root for the underdog, whether it's in sports or politics). But what Ventura was saying made sense to the voters. He spoke about the quality of education for the children of Minnesota, and he complained about lawmakers not returning a $4 billion budget surplus to the citizens of the state.

Even so, Jesse was widely seen as a distant third in the race for the governor's mansion.

In his campaign for governor of Minnesota, Ventura urged fellow Minnesotans to join the Reform Party with this Uncle Sam–style poster. Ventura was the first Reform Party candidate ever to win state office in Minnesota.

It was, perhaps, not the place where he wanted to be. Yet, it was precisely because Ventura's opponents did not consider him a threat that they made their biggest mistake.

Humphrey saw Ventura as a nonfactor in the election, and he refused to debate Coleman on television unless Ventura was also included. Before long, debates were scheduled, and Ventura was included. It was a big boost to Ventura's campaign.

Voters tuning in to the televised debates were able to see the clear contrasts among the candidates. While Humphrey and Coleman continued to say the kinds of things voters had been hearing for years, Ventura was a breath of fresh air. And he was anything but a joke.

If anyone thought that Ventura would arrive at the debates in wrestling trunks and a feather boa, or that he might lift one of the candidates up in the air for a body slam, or that he might rise from his seat and, finger pointing at the camera, launch into a wrestling-style tirade, they were deeply disappointed.

Respectful of the office for which he was running, Ventura wore a business suit to the debates. He came across extremely well to the voters he was trying to win over. While not a career politician, Ventura had spent most of his career in front of the camera, and he was extremely comfortable answering questions off-the-cuff. Perhaps the freshest breath of fresh air, though, was that when Ventura didn't know the answer to a question, he said so.

The message that came across was loud and clear: Jesse Ventura is a concerned Minnesota citizen who may not know all the answers, but he cares deeply about the state and, if elected,

he will work as hard as possible to do the right thing and the best job he can for the people.

A voter can't ask for much more than that.

Suddenly, those who dismissed Ventura as a joke began to take him seriously. In polls statewide, Ventura's numbers began rising. Before long, some polls reported that more than 20 percent of probable voters were saying they would choose Ventura. Still, he wasn't viewed as a major factor in the election. One highly respected state political newsletter was termed generous in predicting that Ventura would receive between 10 and 16 percent of the vote come Election Day.

Gubernatorial candidates Hubert "Skip" Humphrey III, Minnesota's attorney general, and Norm Coleman, mayor of St. Paul, Minnesota, listen to what Ventura has to say during a scheduled debate. Neither Humphrey nor Coleman thought Ventura was likely to win.

Governor-elect Jesse Ventura poses with copies of the Time *magazine bearing his photo.* Time *reprinted 60,000 copies of its Ventura issue due to its popularity, marking only the third time the magazine has gone back to press for an individual issue.*

Humphrey and Coleman continued running typical political campaigns; meanwhile, Ventura continued running his atypical campaign. A television commercial showed a Jesse Ventura action figure fighting Evil Special Interest Man; another showed Jesse posed as Auguste Rodin's famous statue *The Thinker.* (Jesse "The Body" Ventura had told reporters and voters that he wanted to be known as Jesse "The Mind" Ventura.) During the final 72 hours of the campaign, Ventura traveled the length and breadth of the state in a camper, speaking with the people of Minnesota and spreading his message of commonsense politics.

And the people responded. Boy, did they respond!

As Election Day came on November 3, 1998, Minnesota voters showed up to cast their ballots in near-record numbers. When the numbers were all tallied, Ventura had delivered a humiliation to his two opponents that was greater than any he had delivered inside the ring when he was actively wrestling.

Humphrey, long perceived as the front-runner, received 28 percent of the vote, while Coleman received 35 percent. Ventura, meanwhile, captured 37 percent—and the Minnesota governorship.

On CNN, there was laughter and amazement as the result was broadcast. "This is the most bizarre result of the evening," one analyst said.

The *Los Angeles Times* newspaper called Ventura's victory "improbable."

The Associated Press called it "one of the most stunning upsets in U.S. political history."

Time magazine put him on its cover, while Jay Leno welcomed him to *The Tonight Show*.

Meanwhile, a nation of political pundits tried to figure out what it all meant.

Newspaper reporters and broadcasters tripped over themselves to find new ways to express their astonishment that a wrestler—a lowly, comical, ridiculous wrestler, in their view—had attained such a lofty position in national politics. Across the country, in print and on television, reporters, who knew little more about Ventura than that he used to be a wrestler, kept treating his victory as something of a joke.

"A joke?" Ventura responded when asked by the *Los Angeles Times* about being taken seriously as governor. "I don't do anything as

Soon after Ventura's election, a toy manufacturer designed this Jesse Ventura doll, complete with three separate outfits: a governor's suit, a Navy SEAL uniform, and the athletic clothes Ventura wears while volunteering as a football coach for Minnesota's Champlin Park High School.

a joke. I didn't take professional wrestling as a joke. It's a business, and I learned to perform whether injured or sick. It's not a joke to run this state. I take that seriously, and I will."

Such seriousness has prompted many to suggest that Ventura might actually be capable of capturing the presidency in the year 2000—or beyond. During a National Governors' Association meeting in Washington, D.C., in February 1999, Ventura didn't rule out the possibility.

"I could end up down the street here in that big White House, or I could end up living in a hut on the beaches at Kona, where I would throw my watch away and know that when the sun comes up in the morning you get up, when it's straight overhead you eat lunch, and when it goes down, you go to bed."

The quote is a good reflection of who Jesse Ventura is: a man with very deep convictions and a deep streak of independence. Whether as a Navy SEAL, a professional wrestler, a Hollywood actor, or a politician, Jesse Ventura is not a man to be taken lightly.

Those who do wind up as shocked and stunned as Humphrey and Coleman.

VIETNAM TO VENTURA

Jesse Ventura was born James George Janos in Minneapolis, Minnesota on July 15, 1951. His father, George Janos, was a steamfitter for the city of Minneapolis, and his mother, Bernice Janos, worked as a nurse anesthetist. Ventura grew up in the south Minneapolis neighborhood of Longfellow, attended Cooper Elementary School, and graduated from Roosevelt Senior High School in 1969. He served in the navy for six years—four on active duty, two in the naval reserves—and he is a Vietnam veteran. While on active duty, he was a member of Underwater Demolition (SEAL) Team 12. After his discharge from the navy, Ventura attended North Hennepin Community College and then began an 11-year career as a professional wrestler.

While the basics give you a broad sense of where the man born as James George Janos has been in his remarkable life, they are just that: basics. They only provide the broad outline. The details are provided by looking deeper into Ventura's background.

What these basics don't tell you is what it really means to be a Navy SEAL. They don't tell you that after he left military service, he spent six months riding with an outlaw motorcycle club, The Mongols. They don't indicate that while Ventura was

Vietnam veteran Jesse Ventura, shown saluting members of the navy, spent six years in the navy and was trained as a Navy SEAL.

in college, he not only played football, but also acted in a campus production of Aristophanes' *The Birds*.

Ventura's athletic abilities were evident in high school, where he played football and was the captain of the swimming team. But his unique personality was showing even then.

"When I was in high school," Ventura told *USA Today*, "Joe Namath was very popular. He wore white double-breasted suits and fur coats, and I more or less emulated him." One can almost imagine the young James Janos, athletic and outgoing, heading for swimming team practice dressed in his "Broadway" Joe Namath finest!

Upon graduating high school in 1969, Ventura decided that college wasn't in his immediate future, so he chose to trade "Broadway Joe" style duds for military fatigues and follow his brother into the navy. During boot camp, he was shown films about the various services available. One, entitled *Men with Green Faces*, caught his attention. It was about the SEALs, the navy's elite corps of underwater demolition experts.

That's what he wanted to be.

When discussion of Ventura turns to his background, it's often mentioned that he was a U.S. Navy SEAL—which stands for Sea, Air, and Land team. The SEAL teams were officially created in 1962 by order of President Kennedy, who saw a need for American excellence in guerrilla warfare. Before long, the SEALs became known as the best fighting force in the world.

No wonder. The requirements for becoming a SEAL are considerable. SEAL boot camp lasts approximately six months and is generally regarded as one of the toughest, if not the toughest, military training program in the entire world.

How tough? Fully 75 percent of the men who enter SEAL boot camp drop out before the initial training is completed.

Forget, for a moment, the training. Just being accepted into SEAL boot camp is tough. Among the many physical requirements the SEAL hopeful must demonstrate are the ability to complete a minimum of 42 pushups in two minutes, a minimum of 50 situps in two minutes, and a 1.5-mile run in at least 11 minutes and 30 seconds.

After one is accepted into SEAL boot camp, the real work begins. First comes five weeks of progressively more difficult physical conditioning, including running, swimming, calisthenics, and obstacle courses. Two-mile swims wearing swim fins. Four-mile runs. Then comes "Hell Week," five and a half days of physical training with a maximum of four hours of sleep, designed as an ultimate test of the candidates' physical and mental motivation. After that comes three more weeks of physical and classroom training.

That's just phase one.

Phase two consists of seven weeks of training with an emphasis on scuba diving. During the nine weeks of phase three, the SEAL candidate learns skills in demolition, reconnaissance (surveying of enemy territory), infantry tactics, rappelling (descending from steep heights by rope), and more. All along the way, the physical training—running, swimming, and mastering obstacle courses—becomes more and more intense. The distances grow longer, and the times required to complete those distances grow shorter. A two-mile ocean swim, for example, that could be completed in 95 minutes in phase one needs to be completed in 70 minutes in phase three.

The candidate who makes it through phase three then receives additional instruction that can include parachute training and Special Operations Technician training.

Even then, the coveted SEAL classification is six months of probation and service away. That Ventura—or anyone, for that matter—has completed the grueling program is nothing short of incredible.

"I was in the best physical condition of my life," Ventura has often said of his navy service. "My weight was 190 pounds when I went in, and 212 when I came out, and the 22-pound increase was due strictly to things like pushups, situps and running several miles daily in combat boots."

While the details of his military service are known mainly to Ventura and his fellow SEALs, it is widely known that he became proficient in parachuting, jungle warfare, and deep-water dives (he set a personal diving record of 212 feet).

In 1973, after serving in Vietnam, Korea, the Philippines, Hong Kong, Taiwan, and Okinawa, Ventura was honorably discharged from the navy. He returned to the States—and a very different way of life from the one he had known in the service.

"I vowed upon getting out of the military that no one would ever tell me how to dress again," Ventura told a *USA Today* reporter.

Perhaps he also vowed never to take orders again, for he wound up trading in his military garb for biker's clothing and joining an outlaw motorcycle club known as The Mongols. He spent about six months living the biker lifestyle and indulging his love of Harley-Davidsons.

"It was fun for while," he said in 1988, "but it became clear that I would end up in jail."

Returning to Minneapolis, but still seeking direction in his life, Ventura enrolled in North Hennepin Community College. His first semester there, he earned a perfect 4.0 grade point average. He played some football and had brief hopes of a pro gridiron career. He also got a taste of acting when the director of a campus production of Aristophanes' *The Birds* asked him to play the part of Hercules. As Ventura himself admitted, however, he was more or less just killing time. "I was just testing the water. I had no idea of what I really wanted to do."

Then Ventura met an ex-pro wrestler who asked him if he'd ever considered a career in the ring.

"Football is pretty militaristic," Ventura explained in a 1992 interview. "Mentally, I wasn't ready to play professional football. Pro wrestling always appealed to me because of its individuality and the creativity of it."

In fact, it was the persona of 1970s wrestling legend "Superstar" Billy Graham that fueled Ventura's desire to enter the ring.

"When I came home on leave in about 1973 and went to a match at the old Minneapolis Auditorium," Ventura recalled, "that's when I saw Superstar Graham in the flesh and that is when I just looked at him and said, 'I can do what he does.' He was a big influence on how I conducted myself in the ring."

But James Janos needed a ring name. He liked the name "Jesse," but needed a surname to go with it. He looked at a California map, saw the city of Ventura, and thus Jesse Ventura was born.

Now he needed a nickname. Knowing how despised California beachcombers were by middle-American wrestling audiences, Jesse thought he had the perfect hook.

In April 1975 (three months before marrying his wife, Teresa, whom he met in a biker bar), "Surfer" Jesse Ventura made his pro debut in

"Superfly" Jimmy Snuka wrestled in the same Oregon-based promotion as Jesse Ventura. In 1976, he lost the Pacific Northwest heavyweight title to Ventura.

Wichita, Kansas. His opponent was Omar Atlas. Jesse was disqualified for throwing Atlas over the top rope.

It wasn't a particularly auspicious debut, but it was enough for Ventura to know that he had found something he enjoyed doing that would pay the bills.

"Surfer" Jesse wrestled in the Kansas City region for about six months. His style was raw, utilizing a basic power-based attack that leaned heavily toward kicks, punches, body slams, and plenty of attitude. Toward the end of 1975, Ventura accepted an offer to wrestle for the Pacific Northwest promotion, which competed mainly in Portland, Oregon. Three months after arriving in Oregon, Ventura defeated Jimmy Snuka for the Pacific Northwest heavyweight title. Along the way, "Surfer" became "The Body."

After moving from Kansas City to Oregon, Ventura continued westward—to Hawaii. He wrestled in the Aloha State for about seven months, then worked his way back eastward. He returned to Oregon for seven more months, then returned to Minnesota, where he took some of the money he had made in the mat sport, opened a weightlifting gym, and quit professional wrestling.

At the time, it seemed that the partnership between Ventura and professional wrestling had run its course.

It wouldn't be long before "The Body" returned to the ring.

VENTURA IN THE RING

In 1979, Jesse Ventura was making a decent living. He had two gyms, one in San Diego, California, and one in Minneapolis, Minnesota. He didn't have to return to the ring to pay the bills.

But he couldn't stay away.

Portland area promoter Don Owen, a man whom Ventura trusted and respected enormously, called Jesse needing a favor. Owen needed "The Body" to compete in place of another wrestler, who had left the Portland promotion suddenly. Jesse needed to send a promotional videotape to Owen, and he recorded that tape at the television studios of the American Wrestling Association. When Jesse's favor to Owen was complete, the AWA wanted to talk. They thought Ventura had potential.

"It was a major step up for my career," Ventura explained in a 1992 interview, "because in that day, the three major promotions you as a young wrestler wanted to achieve success in were the AWA with Verne Gagne, the Crocketts' promotion based out of Charlotte, which today is basically WCW [World Championship Wrestling], and the WWF [World Wrestling Federation] with Vince McMahon Sr., the eastern seaboard.

In the persona he used as a professional wrestler, Jesse "The Body" Ventura favored leather and snakeskin clothing, wigs, colorful head wraps, and sometimes even feather boas.

WWF World heavy-weight champion Bob Backlund had to defend his title against Ventura several times.

Those were your three money-making territories. Those were your dreams or your goals."

Early in his AWA tenure, Ventura feuded with former National Collegiate Athletic Association (NCAA) weightlifting champion Paul Ellering, who would go on to manage the tag team duo known as the Road Warriors in the mid-80s. However, Ventura didn't really begin to hit his stride until he was matched up with Adrian Adonis as "the East-West Connection."

As a wrestler, Jesse's motto was simple: "Win if you can, lose if you must, but always cheat." As a result, his rather standard wrestling repertoire of body slams, chops to the throat, piledrivers, and bearhugs was accented by eye rakes across the top rope, eye pokes, and chokeholds. His one real finishing move was a backbreaker, a move in which he hoisted his opponent up over his left shoulder and applied enormous pressure that almost always led to a submission.

But Jesse's attraction as a wrestler wasn't his in-ring skills as much as it was his on-microphone persona and his outrageous wardrobe of eye-popping clothes. In one interview tirade, Ventura characterized himself as: "The Body," "the most brutal man in wrestling," "the sickest man in wrestling," "Mr. Money," "Mr. Charisma," and "Mr. Show Business."

All the names fit him very well, particularly "Mr. Charisma." Audiences and television viewers couldn't keep their eyes off "The Body." Wild pink-and-purple tights, multicolored hair, feather boas . . . . One never knew what Ventura was going to wear to the ring next, or what he was going to say next.

"He'd have done better if he'd done a little more wrestling instead of posing," legendary manager Fred Blassie has said of "The Body." The fact is, though, that Ventura didn't do too badly for himself.

After Adonis helped Ventura injure Ellering and drive him out of the AWA, the two men took aim at the AWA World tag team title, then held by Verne Gagne and "Mad Dog" Vachon. On July 20, 1980, Adonis and Ventura became AWA World tag team champions without ever

Legendary manager Fred Blassie was Jesse Ventura's first manager in the WWF.

having to step into the ring! Verne Gagne was vacationing in Europe at the time of the bout and was unable to appear for a scheduled title defense in Denver, Colorado. Adonis and Ventura were awarded the title by default.

Though they didn't win the title in the ring, they proved themselves worthy champions, successfully defending the belts for nearly a year before losing them to the duo of Greg Gagne (Verne's son) and Jim Brunzell on June 14, 1981.

Shortly thereafter, Ventura and Adonis traveled to the WWF, where they signed with manager Fred Blassie, who would go on to manage stars like Hulk Hogan and the Iron Sheik. Rather than place them in immediate tag team competition, Blassie had Ventura and Adonis wrestle in singles matches. Ventura battled Bob Backlund several times for the WWF World heavyweight title, and feuded with "Mr. U.S.A." Tony Atlas.

When Jules and Chief Jay Strongbow won the WWF tag team title in June 1982, Blassie saw his opportunity. He brought Ventura and Adonis together again and secured a series of title matches for his men, but the Strongbows were able to turn back the East-West challenge.

The East-West Connection split up again, and Ventura returned to the AWA, where he concentrated on singles competition. At the time, the AWA World heavyweight champion was Nick Bockwinkel, and the number-one contender to Bockwinkel's title was a relative newcomer to the sport by the name of Hulk Hogan.

Hulk Hogan and Jesse Ventura faced off in a series of AWA matches and arm-wrestling competitions. Later, when Ventura and Hogan were both with the WWF, organizers promoted matches between the two bodybuilders.

AWA fans, who were no friends to Ventura, claimed that "The Body" was afraid of Hogan, who stood in the way of Jesse and an AWA World title shot. Jesse responded by enlisting the assistance of Ken Patera to sideline Hogan for several weeks with a shoulder injury.

Hogan and Ventura finally did wrestle—on Christmas night, 1982—and squared off in a series of arm-wrestling contests through the early months of 1983.

Through 1983 and early 1984, Ventura wrestled in a wide variety of regional promotions around the country, including the Mid-Southern area based in Memphis and the St. Louis area. He feuded with Baron Von Raschke and for a time was managed by "Mouth of the South" Jimmy Hart.

In the middle of 1984, "The Body" received a phone call from WWF head Vince McMahon, who wanted him to return to the federation. At he time, McMahon was making significant moves to expand the WWF from a northeast promotion to a national—and international—promotion. With Hulk Hogan having defeated the Iron Sheik in January 1984, interest in the WWF was expanding at a never-before-seen pace. McMahon wanted to lure wrestlers like Ventura away from small regional promotions to create a federation that was global in scope.

"I was ripe to move, and I was excited about it, to get in on the ground floor," Ventura recalled in 1992. As he said to himself, "If this thing fails, you're probably going to be run out of wrestling. But if it succeeds, you're probably going to get more fame, fortune, and what have you than you'd ever get in your career. So I took the gamble and left."

Ventura immediately targeted WWF World champion Hulk Hogan for title shots, and received favorable treatment from promoters, who saw a match between Hogan and Ventura—two charismatic bodybuilders—as a natural.

After more than nine years of struggling, Ventura had made it to the biggest promotion in the United States, facing the biggest star in the sport in the biggest arenas in the country.

Then tragedy struck.

In September 1984, Jesse began experiencing uncharacteristically severe weakness and shortness of breath. After a match in Oakland, California, he realized he had pain in his upper left lung. A series of tests revealed potentially fatal blood clots on both lungs. Hospitalized, he spent seven days on the critical list. His wrestling career had effectively come to an end. His world was turned upside down.

"I took a look at myself, assessed my position, and decided to make some changes."

VENTURA BEHIND THE MICROPHONE

In an odd way, Jesse Ventura's frightening physical problems might have been the best thing that ever happened to his career. Unable to wrestle, he knew future challenges for World heavyweight championships were now unthinkable.

The notion of concentrating on his biggest assets—his personality and his ability to be comfortable behind the broadcaster's microphone—was not.

During his physical recuperation, Jesse began to work behind the WWF broadcaster's table. It didn't take long for fans and WWF officials alike to realize that the match between Jesse and the microphone was perfect.

Whether he was teamed with Vince McMahon or Gorilla Monsoon, Jesse became a star the likes of which no broadcaster before or since has ever been. He pioneered the notion of the opinionated bad-guy broadcaster, and fans loved it.

But Ventura didn't simply side with the bad guys. He was quick-witted and clever, and he brought to the microphone a deep understanding of what the men inside the ring were dealing with on a physical and competitive level. After all, he himself had dealt with those physical and competitive elements for nearly a decade.

WWF broadcasting personality Jesse "The Body" Ventura appears with Elvira at an April 7, 1986, wrestling event.

In one instance, Jesse commented on a wrestler's rulebreaking tactics by observing, "Now that's smart wrestling."

"It's dirty wrestling, Jesse," McMahon countered.

"Smart wrestling, dirty wrestling, it's winning wrestling."

Indeed, Ventura admired winners more than he admired the bad guys. If a rulebreaker wasn't successful, Ventura had little use for him.

He came up with his own unique nicknames for wrestlers. Tito Santana was "Chico" Santana. Hulk Hogan was "Chump" Hogan. "Hulkamania" was, in Jesse-speak, "Puke-a-mania."

He also delighted in tweaking the pride of the fans in whatever city he happened to be.

One evening, while broadcasting from New Haven, Connecticut, Ventura rhetorically asked, "You know why they built this bridge? So that the people of New Haven can get out of town as quickly as possible!"

Jesse's rise as a broadcaster coincided with the WWF's rise as a federation. So when the WWF pioneered the megaevent WrestleMania in March 1985, there was Ventura at ringside with Gorilla Monsoon, calling all the action. When the WWF returned to network television for the first time in 30 years, as it did on May 11, 1985, with *Saturday Night's Main Event* on the NBC network, there was Ventura at ringside, calling the action along with Vince McMahon.

Whether Ventura was broadcasting on network television or as part of a major pay-per-view event, viewers loved Jesse because Jesse loved what he was doing. He was having fun, it showed, and as a result the viewers had fun, too.

*As a wrestling
commentator in the
WWF, Ventura often
appeared at ringside
to call the action
with WWF president
Gorilla Monsoon.*

"I'm pumped up," he said to Monsoon at the start of WrestleMania II, "'cause I don't have to talk with McMahon, I'm here with you." The not-so-subtle insult at McMahon, head of the WWF, was rare in the 1980s.

Often, if the match wasn't of particular interest, Jesse would turn the conversation to one of his favorite topics: himself. At WrestleMania VI, for example, Ventura observed to Monsoon, "You just remember something, Gorilla, Sean Connery was voted the sexiest man of the year with my hairstyle! I have Paul

Newman's eyes, Kirk Douglas's chin, and Robert Duvall's haircut!"

But when the conversation kept to wrestling and wrestling tactics, as it often did, Jesse's views were crystal clear:

"It ain't cheatin' unless you get caught!" he observed during the WrestleMania V bout between "Macho Man" Randy Savage and Hulk Hogan.

"Those are your rules, Jess," Monsoon responded.

When the WWF begYou can selling videotapes featuring Ventura's commentary without paying him royalties, Ventura took his old federation to court. A federal jury decided the WWF did not have the right to use Jesse's voice without his permission and ruled in favor of "The Body."

"No, those are American rules, the American way."

Whether or not cheating is the American way is certainly open to debate. But an undeniable fact about the American way is that America loves competition.

In the early 1990s, the WWF was beginning to face some very stiff competition in the form of the Atlanta-based WCW organization. Compounding the problem for the WWF was that McMahon was trying to conduct business amidst a wide range of legal allegations, including accusations that he had helped obtain steroids for WWF wrestlers.

By early 1992, the WWF's legal problems were growing—and Ventura was gone. He had joined the rival WCW in a move that, at the time, was seen as a major blow to the WWF's television strength.

Meanwhile, in the wake of the popularity of WrestleMania, the home video market for wrestling videotapes was booming. WrestleMania tapes were among the fastest-selling titles of any kind sold in video stores—movies and concerts included! And not only the WrestleMania events—all kinds of WWF pay-per-view events were appearing on videotape. Tapes were released highlighting special types of matches or particularly popular wrestlers or tag teams.

Jesse's voice was on most of those tapes. And, in his view, he'd never given the WWF permission to use his voice.

A lawsuit was filed. Jesse, arguing that his voice was used on the tapes without his permission, was looking to receive payment of royalties from the sales of videotapes. He asked for $2 million.

According to the WWF's royalty policy at the time, if the WWF released a tape—*The Best of Hulk Hogan*, for example—then Hogan was, of course, entitled to a piece of the profits from the sale of that tape. But, the WWF argued, if the tape was of an event, like WrestleMania, then the profits from the tape needed to be split only between the WWF and the retailer who sold the tape.

The case turned on the fact that Ventura had become a celebrity above and beyond strictly wrestling, due to his involvement in feature films and commercials. The case also pointed out that on a Hulk Hogan tape, royalties were paid to Marvel Comics, because Marvel owned the "Hulk" trademark that Hogan and the WWF used, so the WWF's stated policy was, in fact, incorrect.

On April 13, 1994, Ventura was awarded $809,958 by a federal jury in St. Paul, Minnesota. The verdict was appealed but upheld by the U.S. Court of Appeals Eighth Circuit Court in St. Paul on September 11, 1995.

"Every person I talked to the last two years said I wouldn't be able to beat Vince," Ventura said after the 1994 decision. "Even my wife told me that. But it's a poker game, and I looked at what he had showing and at what I had showing and decided to stay in the game. I felt I was lied to and cheated, and a jury agreed with me."

Jesse fought to defend something he felt was his, something he owned that he believed was used without his permission: his voice, a part of himself that was as unique as his personality, his fingerprints, or his name.

Ah, yes, his name. It's interesting to note that just a few years earlier, on March 31,

1992, Jesse had received ownership of the name "Jesse 'The Body' Ventura" when the U.S. Patent and Trademark Office awarded him registration number 1,681,474.

For Jesse, it made good business sense. After all, you at least need to own your own name if you're going to be a Hollywood star.

5

HOLLYWOOD CALLS

By the time the first WrestleMania was making national headlines in 1985, Jesse Ventura was probably already looking past his career in and around the pro wrestling ring and harboring dreams of big-screen success in Hollywood.

In January 1986, Ventura parlayed his wrestling celebrity into a bit part on the popular television detective show *Hunter*. Though it was only a seven-line part, and he was on screen for less than two minutes, Ventura was featured prominently in the opening scene, and he loved the taste of mainstream acting he'd received. He decided that when the wrestling business had an opportunity that might take him to southern California, he'd be there.

He wouldn't have to wait very long for a bigger taste of acting.

The Hollywood casting agents who were working on a movie called *Predator* were having trouble finding the right physical type to play Sergeant Blain alongside the movie's star, Arnold Schwarzenegger.

Ventura, who was visiting casting directors as often as possible when his business took him to the West Coast, heard about the role. It's said that when "The Body" walked into the

When Hollywood called in the late 1980s, Ventura began his film career, appearing with Arnold Schwarzenegger in Predator *and* The Running Man, *as well as* Batman & Robin.

casting office, the director took one look at Ventura and said, "That's Sergeant Blain!"

While the role of Sergeant Blain gave Ventura his first major Hollywood exposure, it also gave the producers of *Predator* an unanticipated bonus. The movie, which was shot in Mexico in April and May of 1986, featured Sergeant Blain as part of a special military rescue unit that had been sent into the jungles of Latin America to kill an alien.

Ventura's experience as a Navy SEAL was perfect, enabling him to serve as something of an uncredited technical advisor to the film.

"I was able to tell them, 'No, you wouldn't do it that way, you'd do it this way,'" Ventura said of his experience making *Predator*. As a result, the search-and-rescue squad scenes in the movie ring far truer than they otherwise would have had Jesse not been cast in the role.

The movie gave Ventura a classic quotable line, which is slated to be the title of his 1999 autobiography: "I ain't got time to bleed." It also gave Ventura a chance to die on screen, as he is the second member of Schwarzenegger's team to get killed by the alien Predator.

Ventura and Schwarzenegger struck up a fast friendship on the set of *Predator*, perhaps based on their mutual love of bodybuilding, and clearly Arnold admired what Ventura was capable of doing in front of the camera. "He turns out to be a great actor," Schwarzenegger said in 1987, and he backed up his words by securing Ventura the role of Captain Freedom in the 1987 movie *The Running Man*.

As Captain Freedom, Ventura played a brutal fighter turned television commentator and fitness show host. The role was not a very far

cry from his real-life role as wrestler-turned-wrestling commentator, except in this case, the situation is a life-or-death struggle in the bizarre television world of the far future.

"Are you ready for pain?" Ventura growls as Captain Freedom. "Are you ready for suffering? If the answer is yes, then you're ready for Captain Freedom's workout!"

At the time, after appearing alongside Schwarzenegger in two significant movie roles, Ventura was keenly aware of the dangers of becoming typecast. He wanted to avoid being typecast, and he wanted stay in films and avoid working on television.

"If you become too strongly identified with a character, your effectiveness as an actor is diminished. Henry Winkler will be thought of as 'Fonzie' until the day he dies. One actor, in

Ventura, at far right, appeared as Sergeant Blain in the 1987 film Predator, *about an elite military rescue team being stalked by an alien in the jungles of South America. Ventura's experience as a Navy SEAL enabled him to provide valuable technical advice on the film's search-and-rescue scenes.*

particular, who I admire is Robert DeNiro, and he never does television . . . not even talk shows."

Ventura even entertained the idea of comedic roles.

"[My manager] Barry Bloom is excited for me to do comedy," Ventura said in a 1988 interview. "He thinks I have a dry sense of humor that's very marketable. Casting directors have told me the same thing."

In an interview with *USA Today*, Ventura discussed the differences between wrestling and acting as reflected in the contrast between his outlandish wrestling attire and his more conservative leather-and-snakeskin clothing, which he tended to wear around Hollywood. "I can't dress [like a wrestler] anymore and be taken seriously as an actor," he told the newspaper. "I couldn't imagine meeting Roger Ebert, the movie critic, looking like this."

Ventura's first two screen roles were also notable for the fact that they weren't the usual bit parts that wrestlers tend to receive. More than a wrestler appearing as a thug or a bodyguard in a movie, Ventura's roles cast him as a solid supporting actor in major action films.

Unfortunately, his third role was a major step backward.

Ventura appeared as a nameless television commentator in the 1989 bomb *No Holds Barred*, a starring vehicle for Hulk Hogan. The movie was notable mainly for pitting Hogan against a muscular behemoth named Zeus, a match that was echoed off-screen in a pay-per-view event staged by the WWF.

In 1990, Ventura finally got to play comedy—sort of. He scored a minor role as himself in the movie *Repossessed*, a spoof of *The Exorcist* that starred Leslie Nielsen, Ned Beatty, and *Exorcist* star Linda Blair.

Ventura landed his first starring role in 1991's forgotten science fiction flick *Abraxas, Guardian of the Universe*. In the movie, Ventura plays Abraxas, an alien law enforcer who must apprehend a member of his own race who has fled to Earth. (Look for Jesse's son, Tyrell, in a bit part as Willy.) That same year, Ventura had a bit part, as Chewalski, in *Ricochet*, starring Denzel Washington and John Lithgow.

When 1993 rolled around, Ventura once again appeared in a pair of movies. In the virtually unknown *Living and Working in Space: The Countdown Has Begun*, Ventura appeared as DMV Testee. And in the blockbuster movie *Demolition Man*, Ventura appeared as CryoCon.

In *Demolition Man*, Ventura appeared alongside major Hollywood stars Sylvester Stallone, Wesley Snipes, and Sandra Bullock.

The following year, Ventura again returned to comedy with a bit part as White Lightning in 1994's *Major League II*, starring Charlie Sheen, Tom Berenger, and Corbin Bernsen.

In 1996, Ventura made a rare television appearance, as a Man in Black on the 20th episode of the third season of *The X Files* entitled, "Jose Chung's from Outer Space."

In 1997, Ventura and Schwarzenegger were reunited in *Batman & Robin*. Ventura played an Arkham Asylum guard, while Schwarzenegger starred as Mr. Freeze in the big-budget extravaganza.

In an article in the March 1999 edition of *George* magazine, Ventura reflected on the contrasts between professional wrestling and making movies.

Arnold Schwarzenegger became friends with Ventura, a fellow bodybuilder, on the set of Predator, *and chose Ventura for the role of Captain Freedom in his 1987 movie* The Running Man.

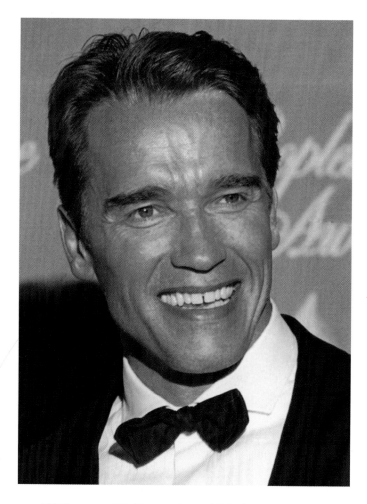

"Sylvester Stallone, Arnold Schwarzenegger—none of them know what it's like to have 20,000 people in the palm of your hand. You control them. You're the manipulator."

While Ventura was making movies and appearing in television shows, he was also thinking about other ways to express his individuality and make his mark on the world.

In 1990, as he was gearing up to play Abraxas, Guardian of the Universe, Ventura began to get upset about a proposed storm sewer and housing project that was threatening the wetlands near his home in Brooklyn Park, Minnesota. So Ventura decided to follow the example of another action film star—Clint Eastwood—and take up a new profession, one at which he would once again achieve remarkable success.

Politics.

6

FROM "THE BODY"
TO "THE MIND"

Brooklyn Park, approximately 10 miles northwest of Minneapolis-St. Paul, is located on the west bank of the Mississippi River. With a population of nearly 60,000, it's the sixth largest city in Minnesota. Parks, trails, and golf courses give the city a lush suburban flavor.

Jesse Ventura wasn't thinking about a career in politics when he decided to run for mayor of Brooklyn Park. He was angry about a zoning decision, and he wanted to do something about it.

If he didn't like the decisions others were making, then maybe he would become the one making the decisions.

Many people thought it was a publicity stunt, but Ventura was deadly serious. On November 6, 1990, Ventura won his first race for public office, defeating 18-year incumbent Mayor Jim Krautkremer by capturing 63 percent of the vote.

"The mayor was the head of the good old boys," Ventura told *George* magazine in 1999. "I always believed that if you're gonna kill the snake, cut off the head."

Ventura's four-year tenure as mayor got mixed reviews. He was out of the office about 20 percent of the time, working on movies like *Demolition Man* and *Major League II*. During political meetings with members of the city council, he engaged in

Jesse Ventura began his political career in 1990 by running for mayor of Brooklyn Park, the sixth-largest city in Minnesota. Ventura served as mayor until 1995 and made crime reduction a top priority.

pro wrestling-style theatrics that resulted in at least one lawsuit for slander (a judge later dismissed the case) and caused the Brooklyn Park *Sun Post* to write an editorial urging Ventura to resign his office.

"It was a three-ring circus," said one city council member who served during Ventura's term as mayor. "I don't want to comment," said another. "He's a very vindictive person."

On the positive side of his legacy, Ventura took a strong interest in lowering crime, and the crime rate did fall during his time as mayor. Taxes didn't go up. He also made a trip to Washington, D.C., that was credited with helping win federal funding for a highway extension.

In 1991, Ventura was profiled on *Lifestyles of the Rich and Famous*. He was asked where he would go next after being mayor. His response, ironically, was: "Maybe senator next. Or maybe governor. And then who knows, maybe in the year 2000 it will be Jesse Ventura for president. Now wouldn't that be something to think about?"

Toward the end of his term as mayor, the city council launched an investigation into the question of whether or not Ventura actually lived in Brooklyn Park. At the time, about four months before he would no longer be mayor, Ventura had purchased another home in a nearby suburb, his Brooklyn Park home was for sale, and his children had already been enrolled in their new school. A judge ruled that he could complete his term, because while the family didn't all live in the Brooklyn Park home, Jesse stayed there occasionally.

When he left the mayor's office, Jesse continued his stint as a radio broadcaster for KFAN in Minneapolis. He held down a three-hour air-shift five days a week, Mondays through Fridays from 10 A.M. to 1 P.M.

Then he was approached by the Reform Party and asked to run for governor. It took Ventura a year to decide to run, a year of being pressured by Reform Party representatives, a year of soul-searching both within his own mind and in discussions with his wife and children.

When the year was over, he made a decision that would not only make history, but respect history.

"Politician is not necessarily a bad word," Ventura said in the April 1999 issue of *Esquire* magazine. "I've always drawn the line between being a politician and being a career politician. I just believe that the forefathers of this country, they wanted everyone to be qualified to get elected. They didn't want it to be elitist. They wanted the butcher, the baker, and the candlestick maker. They'd all be qualified, and then you'd go back to what you did."

Indeed, it was a theme that Jesse echoed throughout the campaign. One he had to echo, in fact, if he wanted to win. After all, he was running against a pair of heavyweight politicians: Republican Norm Coleman, the popular mayor of St. Paul, and Democrat Hubert H. Humphrey III, the son of the former vice president of the United States.

"Go to the secretary of state's office," Ventura told *Newsweek* when asked about his qualifications for being governor. "It says: live in the state for a year and be over 25. That's it. I think that's what the Founding Fathers wanted."

The Ventura campaign was a wild one, seen by many at first as being a sideshow to the

Ventura used his charisma and experience as a wrestling broadcaster to become a radio talk show host in Minnesota. Working in radio helped him get in touch with the people of Minnesota and paved the way for his run for governor.

political main event. But when support for Ventura kept growing and growing, Coleman and Humphrey—and the voters of Minnesota—began to take him seriously.

Ventura spoke about eliminating state property taxes and about returning a $4 billion state budget surplus to the voters. His slogan was "Retaliate in '98," a reference to his being an outsider running against established politicians. When he appeared on television in debates against the other two candidates, he was a refreshing contrast—especially when he admitted on occasion that he really didn't know very much about this particular issue or that one.

"Why would people think that [my opponents] are any more qualified than me?" *George* magazine reported Ventura as saying. "I've done things that would make both of them wet their pants." It wasn't clear whether Jesse was referring to his Navy SEAL days, his biker club days, his wrestling days, or all three.

"The key to his appeal is aimed at people's anger at managed politics," Harry Boyte, a political analyst at the University of Minnesota, told the *Los Angeles Times*. "He aimed at the feeling that political advertising was condescending, that Democrats and Republicans were condescending to the people. 'He is like us, and we are not as stupid as they think,' is the message the voters were sending, and not just to Minnesota."

"It's a case of the politicians being a bit pompous and arrogant and underestimating the voters," Ventura agreed. "Minnesotans know Minnesotans."

Still, the reaction to Ventura's election was nothing short of stunning. CNN news anchors actually laughed while reporting the result on election night, saying, "This is the most bizarre result of the evening." Newspapers and wire services scrambled to find new synonyms for "upset," "astonishing," and "incredible."

"How shocking was his victory?" asked the *Los Angeles Times*. "To borrow imagery from his former professions: Ventura took on an established political tag team, hoisted his opponents over his head, twirled them around the political ring and slammed them headfirst to the canvas. Only this time, the blood was not fake."

"Now I know what Saddam Hussein felt like when those bombs started falling," said Humphrey.

"The people of Washington could not be more surprised if Fidel Castro came loping across the Midwestern prairie on the back of a hippopotamus," said CBS news anchor Dan Rather.

Even President Bill Clinton commented on Ventura's election, saying, "I think you're going to have a lot of politicians spending time in the gym now."

White House press secretary Joe Lockhart said that he "never thought that 'bodyslam' would become a literal phrase in politics."

Lockhart's reference to Ventura's nickname—"The Body"—was a bit out of date, however. Jesse had decided on the campaign trail that he was trading in one nickname for another. He now wanted to be known as Jesse "The Mind" Ventura.

In the wake of the election, national magazines scrambled to feature articles on the new governor. Every article seemed to concentrate in large part on Jesse's wrestling career, a fact that irritated the governor.

"I haven't wrestled in 12 years," Ventura told *Newsweek.* "And anyway, I'm not some big, dumb wrestler. I know wrestlers who pay more in taxes than most people make. How can they be dumb? Wrestling is ballet with violence. They don't call Nureyev dumb."

"He is a man of great discipline," observed Arnold Schwarzenegger, who attended Ventura's inauguration. "He will do a good job if the politicians leave him alone."

During his inauguration speech, Jesse reached back to his Navy SEAL days as a way of setting the stage for the future:

> Well, I told you I was going to come here today and was going to speak from the heart. Well, not totally true. I have to read something. And yes, when you get 47, these [eyeglasses] become a part of your uniform.

Ventura and his running mate Mae Schunk, a teacher of 36 years, celebrate their victory on election night November 3, 1998.

But I received this just a little while ago. And it says a lot to me, and so for all you people out there who have questions on whether I can succeed, questions whether I can do a good job on this huge task, the big shoes I have to follow in, the row of them sitting there in the second row that have come before me.

I received this yesterday and it says: 'I'm sure you must be nervous and apprehensive and maybe a little frightened by such a huge and challenging endeavor. But keep this in mind, you've been there. You've been pushed, tried and tested by the best, and you've passed with flying colors. Keep that "hooyah" spirit and don't change a thing. I wish you the very best of luck and success. Sincerely, Master Chief Terry "Mother" Moy.'

So for any of you that have any doubts, he's standing to the left of me and I'll behave.

And it touched me a great deal because as I move forward, I know I can always look back to my Navy SEAL training when the going gets tough, and I know it's not as tough as that. And that's what this is all about again, is simply doing your best.

It was a theme that Ventura brought up time and again during the campaign—that if elected, he would do his best. But as the celebration of the election gave way to the business of the state, and as Ventura began to make policy decisions and high-profile public appearances, some people began to wonder whether Minnesotans had done their best on election day.

"I'm less worried as time goes by," former Minnesota Governor Al Quie told *Esquire* magazine, "because of the people he's appointed so

Jesse Ventura is sworn in as the 38th governor of Minnesota while his wife Terry, at left, and daughter, Jade, center, watch. In his inaugural speech Ventura vowed to do his best and quoted his former Navy SEAL trainer, Master Chief Terry Moy.

far. Put in quality people, and you can get away with a lot of ineptitude. But I can't tell you how many people have called me since the election and told me, 'Al, I'd never have voted for him if I thought he'd win.'"

Even those record numbers of Minnesota voters who cast their ballots for Ventura had to wonder about Jesse's judgement when he made an appearance on *The Late Show with David Letterman* shortly after his election. Letterman asked Ventura to choose which city he liked best, Minneapolis or St. Paul. Ventura chose Minneapolis, commenting before a national television audience, "Have you been to St. Paul? Whoever designed the streets must have been drunk. I think it was those Irish guys. You know what they like to do."

It wasn't the kind of joke a career politician would have made, and while some Minnesotans might have agreed with the governor's views, others didn't, and took the opportunity to loudly say so. As is unfortunately often the case in politics, a silly comment got blown out of proportion, prompting Governor Ventura to issue the following statement:

> "If I offended anyone, I apologize. *The David Letterman Show* is a show of comedy. It's a show that has 'Top Ten Lists' and is generally considered comedic and that's the light in which I did the show was to go on there and have fun.
>
> The city of St. Paul is a tremendous city. When I talked about the streets it was simply me remembering back when I used to wrestle at the [St. Paul] Civic Center and I would always try to beat the crowd out of the Civic Center, if it was possible. And it never failed, every three weeks I'd take a wrong

turn and I would spend a great length of time trying to find the freeway.

And it was just me. It was something in my life that went on and that's in light of what it was meant when I was on the show.

Also today I had a heartwarming experience of having a group of ninth-graders from Deer River, Minnesota, in here and I opened for questions from one of the ninth-graders and the ninth-grader asked me, 'Mister Governor, don't they get it?'

And I said, 'Get what?'

And they said, 'That you were on *David Letterman*, that that's comedy and you were just there having fun and making jokes.'

And I said, 'No,' I said, 'but I'm glad you ninth-graders do.'

And so, you know, the point is that I'm always enlightened by young people. They're the ones that make me feel very good about doing the job I do because they are extremely intelligent.

Finally, it does sadden me greatly, though, that the Minneapolis–St. Paul and Minnesota that I grew up in and spent my life in had a sense of humor and apparently today the Minneapolis–St. Paul and Minnesota that I live in does not. And those are my statements on that, and as I said, that does not make me feel good that we've somehow lost our sense of humor; apparently we have.

But again I apologize if anyone was offended. It wasn't meant to be offensive at all. It was simply doing *The David Letterman Show* and that show is based on comedy and laughter and humor and, you know, people have obviously took it the wrong way and I'll know better next time to be more sullen and straightforward if I do one of those shows.

Of course, "sullen and straightforward" is not the Jesse Ventura way. He is a man who has always spoken his mind, regardless of whether it was politically correct or not, and he's not likely to change anytime soon. Minnesotans can expect several more years of interesting state politics.

Still, when all is said and done, it must be said that Jesse Ventura's election as governor does truly fulfill the American dream that hard work and determination pay off, that anyone can grow up to be—well, if not president (yet), then at least governor of the 12th largest state in the union. Jesse Ventura is living proof that, truly, anything is possible in this great land of ours.

And the Jesse Ventura story is far from over. So many questions remain: Will his tenure as governor be a successful one? Will he be reelected? Will he run for national office? Will he quit politics and return to Hollywood? Or will he choose another career path completely and astound the world anew?

There's only one answer, to borrow Ventura's enthusiastic cry indicating "onward and upward, no matter what the odds" from his Navy SEAL days:

"Hooyah!"

Chronology

1951   Born James George Janos in Minneapolis, Minnesota, on July 15.

1969   Becomes a U.S. Navy SEAL.

1973   Receives an honorable discharge from the navy.

1975   Makes his pro wrestling debut.
Marries wife, Teresa.

1980   With Adrian Adonis, is awarded the AWA World tag team title by default.

1981   Loses AWA World tag team title to Greg Gagne and Jim Brunzell.

1982   Wrestles Hulk Hogan for the first time in the AWA.

1984   Hospitalized to treat blood clots in both lungs.

1987   Appears as Sergeant Blain in the movie *Predator* and as Captain Freedom in *The Running Man*.

1990   Elected mayor of Brooklyn Park, Minnesota.

1993   Plays CryoCon in the movie *Demolition Man*.

1998   Elected governor of Minnesota.

1999   Publishes his autobiography *I Ain't Got Time to Bleed: Reworking the Body Politic from the Bottom Up*.

Further Reading

Anderson, Steve. "Mind over Matter: The Day Jesse Became the Governing Body." *Inside Wrestling* (March 1999): 38–41.

Gray, Paul. "Body Slam." *Time* 152, no. 20 (November 16, 1998): 1–4.

Pattison, Kermit. "Pinning Jesse Down." *George* (March 1999): 92–95, 124–125.

Pierce, Charles P. "The First Hundred Hours." *Esquire* 131 (April 1999): 100–105.

Tapper, Jake. *Body Slam: The Jesse Ventura Story.* New York: St. Martin's Press, 1999.

Ventura, Jesse. *I Ain't Got Time to Bleed.* New York: Random House, 1999.

Index

Photo Credits

Archive Photos: pp. 40, 43; Associated Press/Wide World Photos: pp. 6, 9, 11, 12, 14, 16, 24, 32, 36, 46, 48, 52, 55, 56, 60; Courtesy of the Minnesota Governor's Office: p. 1; Jeff Eisenberg Sports Photography: pp. 22, 26, 28, 29, 35.

MATT HUNTER has spent 18 years writing about professional wrestling. In addition to this biography of Jesse Ventura, the author has written *Superstars of Pro Wrestling* and a biography of Hulk Hogan. He has also interviewed countless wrestlers on national television, photographed innumerable bouts from ringside, and written more magazine articles about the mat sport than he cares to calculate.